Street in Venice
Mitchell Wolf
Regular and Large Print Cross Stitch Pattern

Serenity Stitchworks
www.SerenityStitchworks.com

A PowerHouse Imaging, Ltd. Company

© 2020 PowerHouse Imaging, Ltd

www.SerenityStitchworks.com

All rights reserved

Street in Venice

Pattern Details

Design Size:
189w x 324h stitches

Types of Stitches:
Full stitches only, no half or quarter stitches, no backstitching

Level of Difficulty:
Advanced

Sewn Design Size:
14 count: 13.50 x 23.14 inches - 343mm x 588mm
18 count: 10.50 x 18.00 inches - 267mm x 457mm
20 count: 9.45 x 16.20 inches - 240mm x 411mm
22 count: 8.59 x 14.73 inches - 218mm x 374mm

Fabric size necessary for design:
Add six inches to both length and width (3" on each side)

Number of floss colors:
76 (DMC cotton floss) No blended colors.

Become a member of the Serenity Stitchworks Community and receive tips, tricks, fun facts and free cross stitch patterns. Go to **www.SerenityStitchworks.com** and sign up today.

Instructions for Advanced Fine-Art Cross Stitch

You have in your hands (or on your computer screen) what is referred to as an "advanced fine-art cross stitch" project. Unlike individual objects in a cross stitch design such as flowers, teddy bears, hearts, etc., you will be covering the entire canvas with stitches. You are painting with thread!

The following instructions will give you advice on the best methods to use in completing this type of design. Have fun with it – the type of stitch you will use is simple and is the same as one would use in any cross stitch project.

1. When you purchase the fabric for your project, allow a minimum of 3 extra inches on all four sides of the pattern. For example, if your finished design is 12" x 14" you would purchase an 18" x 20" piece of fabric. Finish the edges of the piece with either a serging stitch, zig zag stitch or masking tape. This will prevent the fabric from raveling.

2. The next and VERY IMPORTANT step is to mark grid lines on your fabric. Mark the grid lines to match the grid lines of the pattern. These designs are created with ten stitches per square in the grid of the pattern – both vertically and horizontally.

    The best product we have found to mark the grid lines is the "Easy-Count Guideline." It will not disappear as you put your stitches in and will remain on top of your stitches. And, it will save you hours of time. If you cannot find this in your local needlework shop, you can order it online.

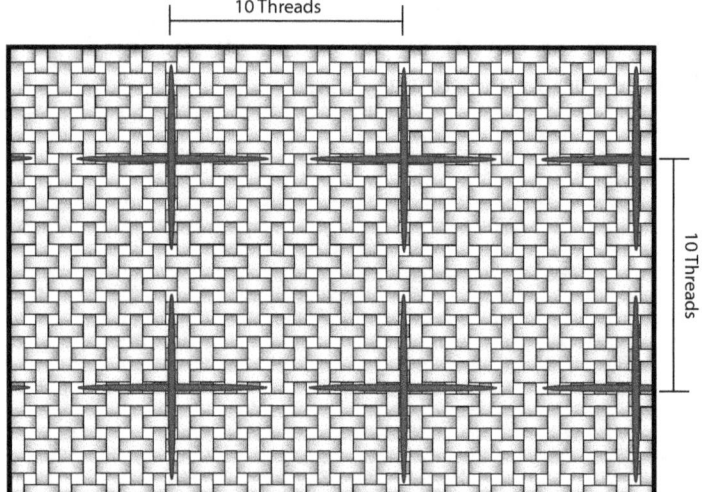

3. Purchase all the floss you will need before you begin, wind the floss on floss bobbins (don't stretch the floss) and put the floss number on each bobbin. Arrange the floss bobbins numerically in a bobbin case and put only the floss used in the design in the box. Not only will you get to see the whole array of colors you will use in your design, you will also have all of the floss there so you won't have to stop in the middle of your design to pick up a needed color.

4. We recommend using a hoop, but if you prefer stitching without one that's okay too. We have found the "Morgan No-Slip Hoop" to be the best. It has a patented tongue-in-groove design that holds the fabric firmly in place with a long enough screw to allow the needed expansion. It also doesn't leave as much of an imprint on your fabric – don't know exactly why, but think it is probably because of the tongue-in-groove design. If you cannot find this product in your local needlework shop, you can order it online.

    You may want to try our "Reverse Hoop Method" where you put the outer ring of your hoop on the back side of your fabric and the inner ring on the top. It takes a bit getting used to, but it will keep your piece cleaner, you will be able to start and stop with your thread right up to the edge of the hoop, and the right side of your stitches will not have the stress as you put your piece in the hoop.

5. Now you are ready to begin stitching. Make sure your hands are clean whenever you work with your project.

Begin in the upper left-hand corner of the design and work either vertically or horizontally as you complete your stitches. To begin stitching, thread your needle with 2 strands of floss for stitch counts of 14 to 20 stitches per inch. If you are using a canvas with a higher stitch count (25 stitches per inch and up) and you are stitching over one thread, you will use 1 strand of floss.

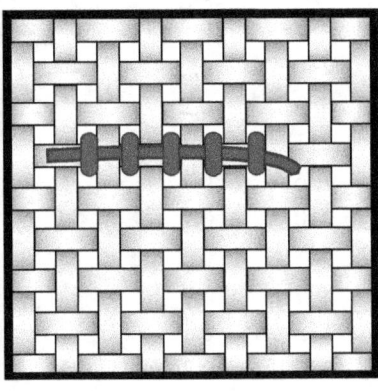

When making your first few stitches, leave a 2 cm tail at the back of your work. Hold this tail so that your first few stitches are worked over it. This secures your thread. Never tie a knot in your thread. See how this is done in the diagram. As your project progresses, you will be able to anchor your thread on the back side of the already completed stitches.

6. Cross stitch is worked in even, slanted stitches as you will see in the diagram. The stitches used to make a cross

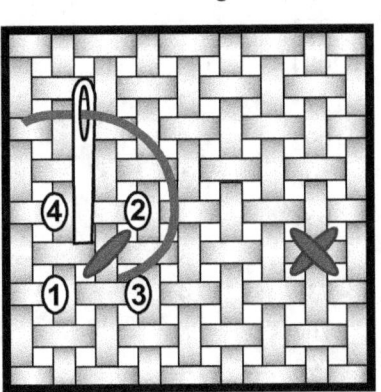

stitch are usually done diagonally from left to right, laying down the first half of the cross and then back from right to left to complete the cross. See diagram.

All the stitches MUST be completed the same way (the first stitch of the cross always in the same direction and the second stitch of the cross always in the same direction) – this is very important – if you don't make the stitches consistent, your project will not look beautiful as you had planned.

When stitching, keep the tension of your thread even and do not pull too tight – just tight enough for the thread to lie evenly on the fabric.

7. When doing an advanced fine-art design such as this, it is recommended that you complete each square before moving unto the next. By doing this, the second half of the stitch will always be completed and not accidentally forgotten, and you will have a firmer finished product.

8. Use the "stab" or the "push and pull" method for doing your cross stitches. We do not recommend the "sewing method," which is done by the needle going in the front of the fabric, out the back and into the front again in one motion. The reason for this is that it would have to be done without a hoop, and the stitches become uneven. Also, with this type of a design (advanced fine-art), floss colors change frequently with just a few stitches done in a particular color.

Skein Conversion Chart

Use this chart if you are using a thread count smaller or larger than 18 count to determine how much floss you will need.

Fabric Count	500 stitches	1,000 stitches	2,000 stitches	3,000 stitches	4,000 stitches	5,000 stitches	6,000 stitches	7,000 stitches	8,000 stitches	9,000 stitches	10,000 stitches
11 count Aida - 4 strands	3/4	1 1/2	3	4 1/2	5 3/4	7 1/4	8 3/4	10	11 1/2	13	14 1/2
14 count Aida - 3 strands	1/2	1	1 3/4	3	3 1/2	4 1/4	5 1/4	6	6 3/4	7 3/4	8 1/2
16 count Aida - 2 strands	1/4	1/2	1	1 1/2	2	2 1/2	3	3 1/2	4	4 1/2	5
18 count Aida - 2 strands	1/4	1/2	1	1 1/2	1 3/4	2 1/4	2 3/4	3 1/4	3 1/2	4	4 1/2
20 Count Aida - 1 strand	1/4	1/2	1	1 1/4	1 3/4	2	2 1/2	2 3/4	3 1/4	3 3/4	4
22 count Hardanger - 1 strand	1/4	1/2	3/4	1 1/4	1 1/2	2	2 1/4	2 1/2	3	3 1/4	3 3/4

Number of skeins.

Street in Venice

Key

Position	Symbol	Cat. No.	Brand	Type	Stitches	Skeins
1	A	Blanc	D.M.C.	Stranded Cotton	791	0.4
2	B	B5200	D.M.C.	Stranded Cotton	365	0.2
3	C	Ecru	D.M.C.	Stranded Cotton	644	0.3
4	D	167	D.M.C.	Stranded Cotton	497	0.3
5	E	169	D.M.C.	Stranded Cotton	280	0.2
6	F	310	D.M.C.	Stranded Cotton	383	0.2
7	■	317	D.M.C.	Stranded Cotton	211	0.1
8	⊠	370	D.M.C.	Stranded Cotton	136	0.1
9	▲	371	D.M.C.	Stranded Cotton	210	0.1
10	Ⅳ	415	D.M.C.	Stranded Cotton	543	0.3
11	★	422	D.M.C.	Stranded Cotton	899	0.4
12	▲	435	D.M.C.	Stranded Cotton	175	0.1
13	—	437	D.M.C.	Stranded Cotton	530	0.3
14	⊘	451	D.M.C.	Stranded Cotton	424	0.2
15	✳	452	D.M.C.	Stranded Cotton	598	0.3
16	⊠	453	D.M.C.	Stranded Cotton	759	0.4
17	◧	535	D.M.C.	Stranded Cotton	281	0.2
18	◆	543	D.M.C.	Stranded Cotton	619	0.3
19	H	610	D.M.C.	Stranded Cotton	1090	0.5
20	I	611	D.M.C.	Stranded Cotton	973	0.5
21	J	612	D.M.C.	Stranded Cotton	2084	0.9
22	K	613	D.M.C.	Stranded Cotton	1573	0.7
23	L	640	D.M.C.	Stranded Cotton	1092	0.5
24	M	644	D.M.C.	Stranded Cotton	708	0.3
25	●	645	D.M.C.	Stranded Cotton	651	0.3
26	#	646	D.M.C.	Stranded Cotton	544	0.3
27	▣	647	D.M.C.	Stranded Cotton	737	0.4
28	▲	648	D.M.C.	Stranded Cotton	1767	0.8
29	=	676	D.M.C.	Stranded Cotton	798	0.4
30	♥	677	D.M.C.	Stranded Cotton	386	0.2
31	::	729	D.M.C.	Stranded Cotton	238	0.1
32	✚	738	D.M.C.	Stranded Cotton	1248	0.6
33	⬥	739	D.M.C.	Stranded Cotton	785	0.4
34	‡	744	D.M.C.	Stranded Cotton	618	0.3
35	Y	745	D.M.C.	Stranded Cotton	506	0.3
36	◎	746	D.M.C.	Stranded Cotton	461	0.2
37	N	762	D.M.C.	Stranded Cotton	583	0.3
38	O	822	D.M.C.	Stranded Cotton	194	0.1
39	P	838	D.M.C.	Stranded Cotton	499	0.3
40	Q	839	D.M.C.	Stranded Cotton	1631	0.7
41	R	840	D.M.C.	Stranded Cotton	955	0.4
42	S	841	D.M.C.	Stranded Cotton	716	0.3
43	≫	842	D.M.C.	Stranded Cotton	1724	0.8

Street in Venice

Key

Position	Symbol	Cat. No.	Brand	Type	Stitches	Skeins
44	▬	844	D.M.C.	Stranded Cotton	366	0.2
45	⋈	869	D.M.C.	Stranded Cotton	252	0.2
46	⊡	928	D.M.C.	Stranded Cotton	316	0.2
47	Σ	934	D.M.C.	Stranded Cotton	1963	0.9
48	✿	935	D.M.C.	Stranded Cotton	392	0.2
49	⊞	945	D.M.C.	Stranded Cotton	322	0.2
50	$	951	D.M.C.	Stranded Cotton	1503	0.7
51	Ψ	3021	D.M.C.	Stranded Cotton	1373	0.6
52	╱	3022	D.M.C.	Stranded Cotton	729	0.4
53	⊞	3023	D.M.C.	Stranded Cotton	1627	0.7
54	Ω	3024	D.M.C.	Stranded Cotton	419	0.2
55	T	3032	D.M.C.	Stranded Cotton	2473	1.1
56	U	3033	D.M.C.	Stranded Cotton	823	0.4
57	V	3045	D.M.C.	Stranded Cotton	757	0.4
58	W	3046	D.M.C.	Stranded Cotton	483	0.3
59	X	3047	D.M.C.	Stranded Cotton	644	0.3
60	Y	3072	D.M.C.	Stranded Cotton	666	0.3
61	▲	3078	D.M.C.	Stranded Cotton	549	0.3
62	XII	3371	D.M.C.	Stranded Cotton	2131	0.9
63	•>	3782	D.M.C.	Stranded Cotton	1356	0.6
64	⌐	3787	D.M.C.	Stranded Cotton	854	0.4
65	⧖	3790	D.M.C.	Stranded Cotton	1479	0.7
66	⊡	3823	D.M.C.	Stranded Cotton	1216	0.6
67	⋕	3827	D.M.C.	Stranded Cotton	326	0.2
68	4	3854	D.M.C.	Stranded Cotton	477	0.2
69	✕	3855	D.M.C.	Stranded Cotton	737	0.4
70	⸚	3860	D.M.C.	Stranded Cotton	228	0.1
71	◀	3861	D.M.C.	Stranded Cotton	281	0.2
72	◼	3862	D.M.C.	Stranded Cotton	1100	0.5
73	2	3863	D.M.C.	Stranded Cotton	724	0.4
74	3	3864	D.M.C.	Stranded Cotton	1921	0.9
75	6	3865	D.M.C.	Stranded Cotton	980	0.5
76	7	3866	D.M.C.	Stranded Cotton	863	0.4

Regular Print Chart

Street in Venice - Regular Print

Overview

Fabric: Aida White

Stitch Count: 71/100mm   or   18.0/inch

Chart Size: 189 x 324 Stitches

Finished Size: 267 x 457 mm   or   10.5 x 18.0 inch

Fabric Size: 417 x 607 mm   or   16.4 x 23.9 inch

Stitch Style: Cross stitch - 2 strands

Below is a plan showing how the chart pages fit together.
The page number is shown at the top left of each chart page.

A:1	B:1	C:1	D:1
A:2	B:2	C:2	D:2
A:3	B:3	C:3	D:3
A:4	B:4	C:4	D:4
A:5	B:5	C:5	D:5

Position A:1 — Street in Venice - Regular Print

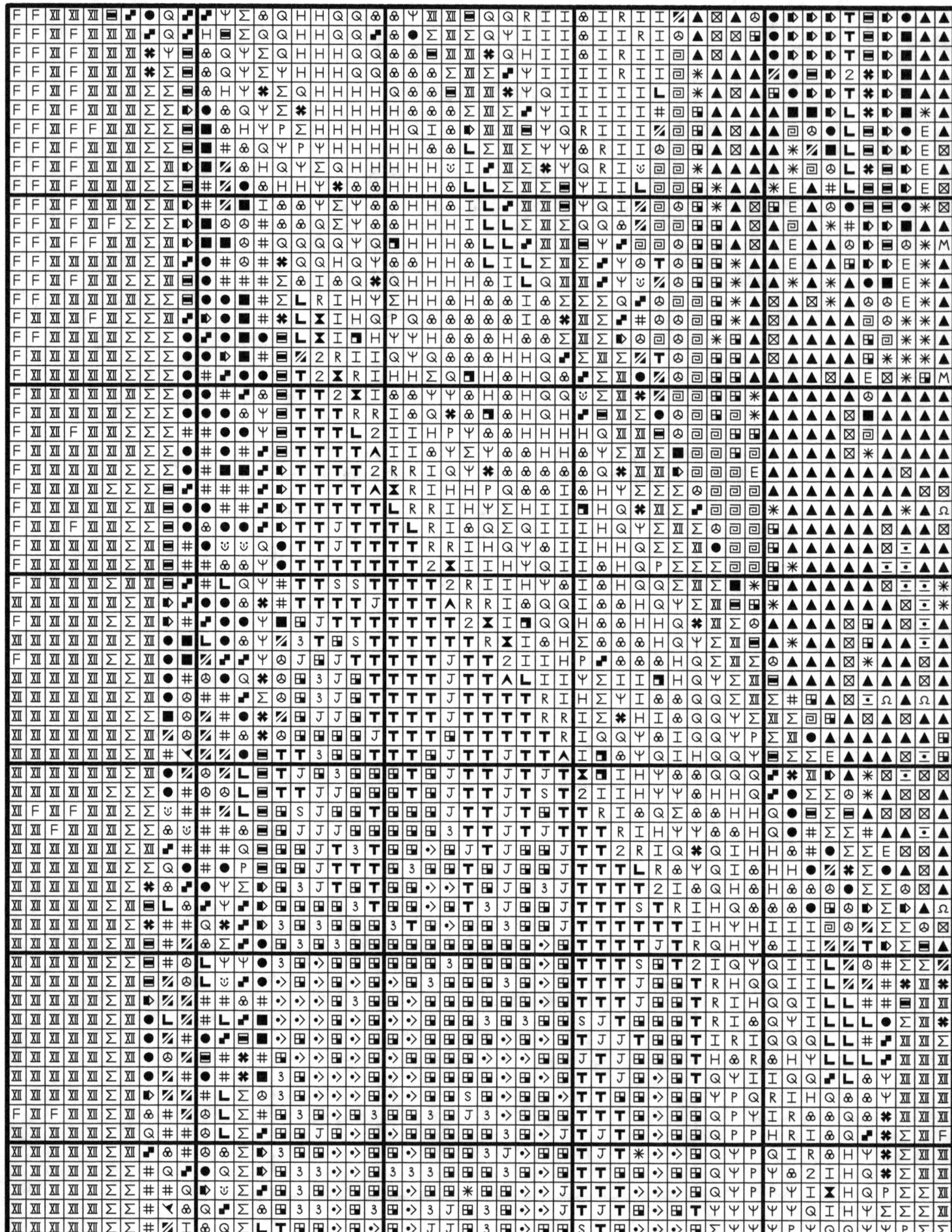

Position B:1 — Street in Venice - Regular Print

Position C:1 — Street in Venice - Regular Print

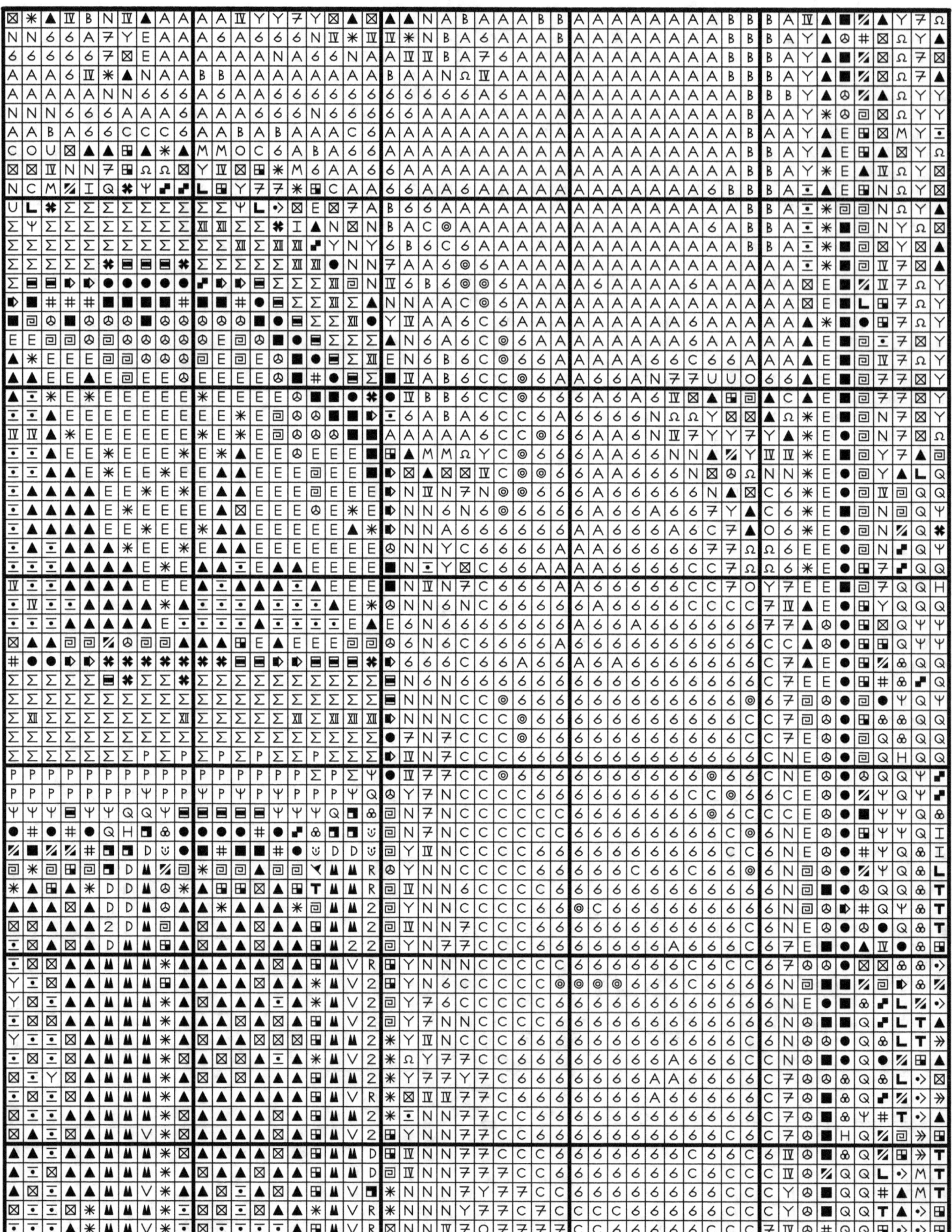

Position D:1 — Street in Venice - Regular Print

Position A:2 — Street in Venice - Regular Print

Position B:2 — Street in Venice - Regular Print

Position C:2 — Street in Venice - Regular Print

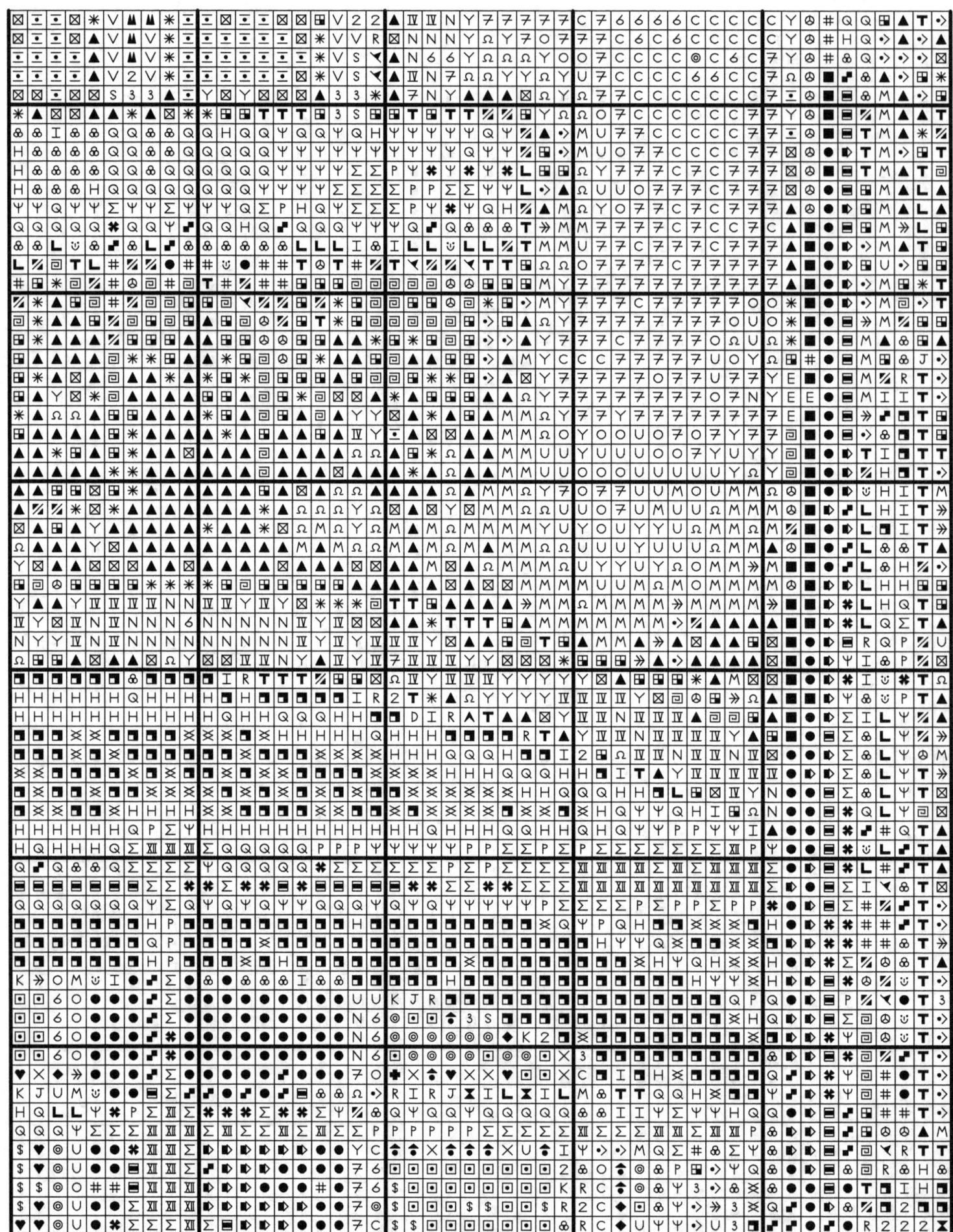

Position D:2 — Street in Venice - Regular Print

Position A:3

Street in Venice - Regular Print

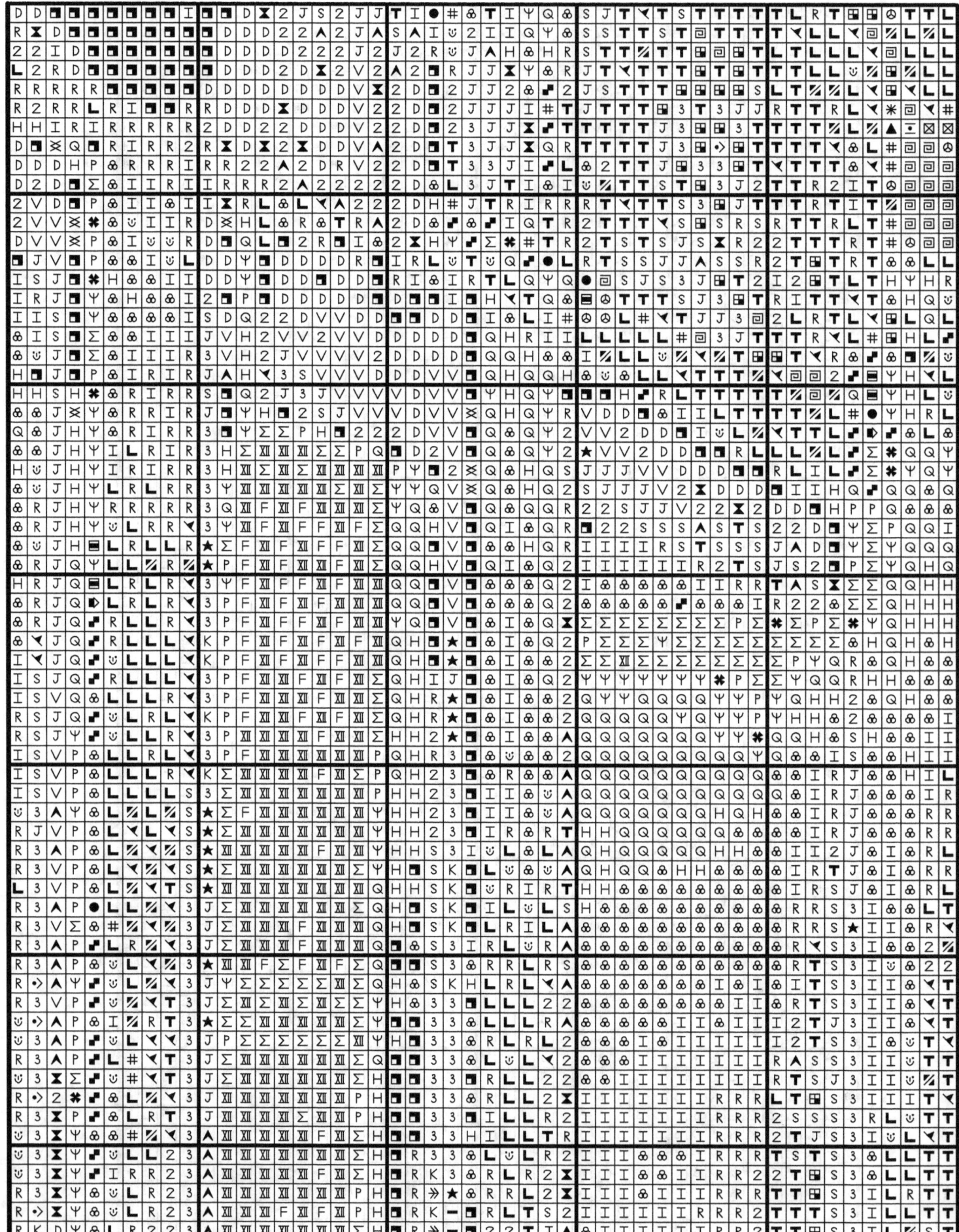

Position C:3 — Street in Venice - Regular Print

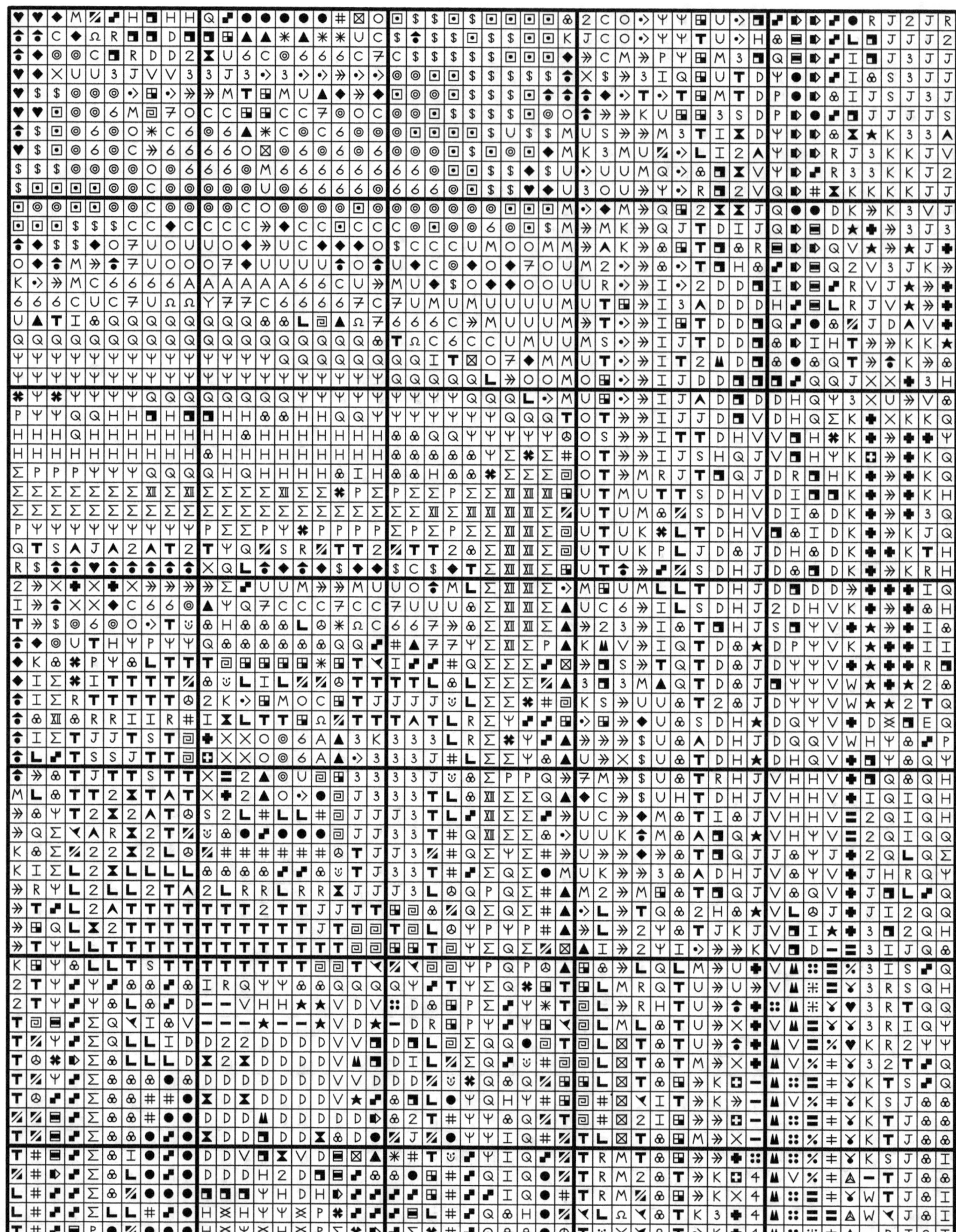

18

Position D:3 — Street in Venice - Regular Print

Position A:4 Street in Venice - Regular Print

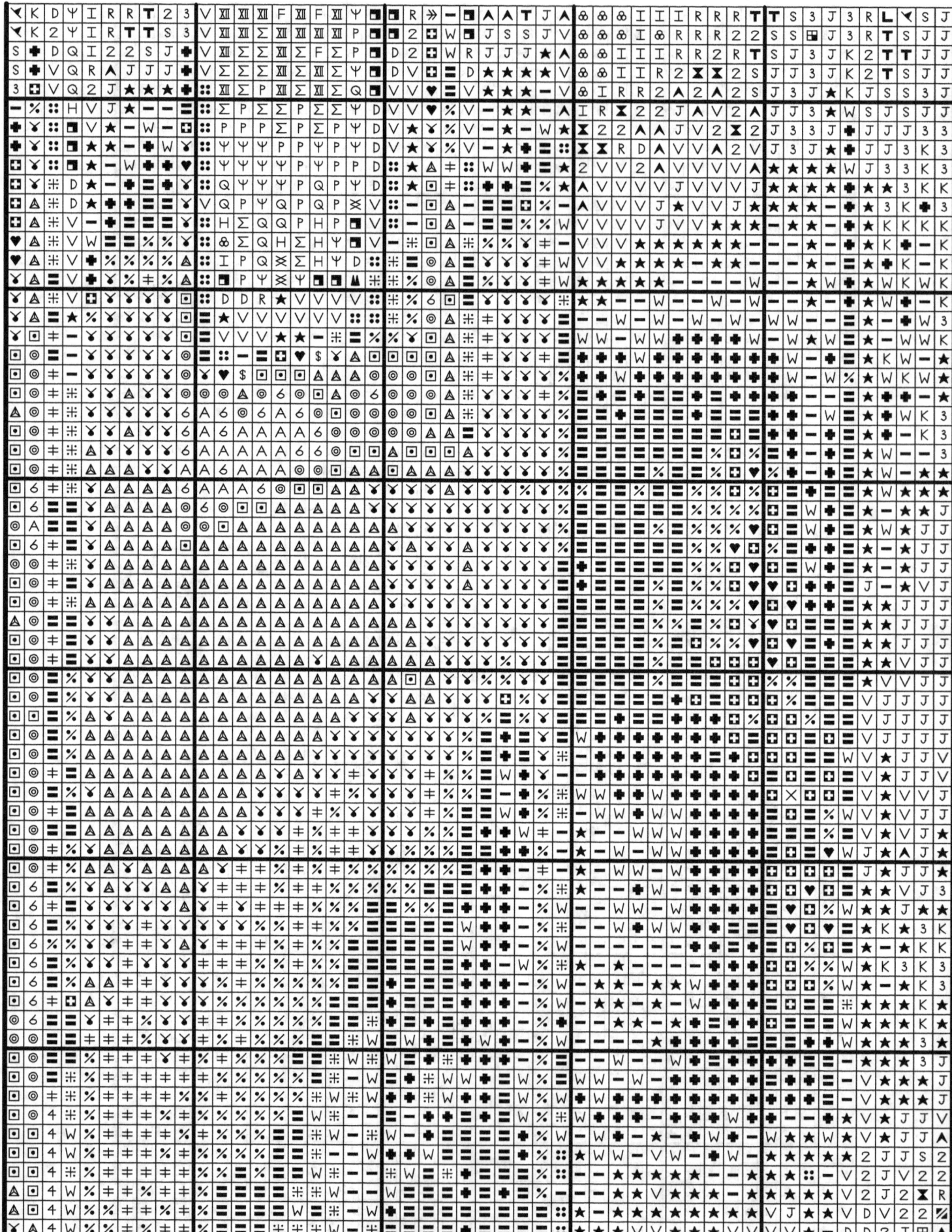

Position B:4 — Street in Venice - Regular Print

Position C:4 — Street in Venice - Regular Print

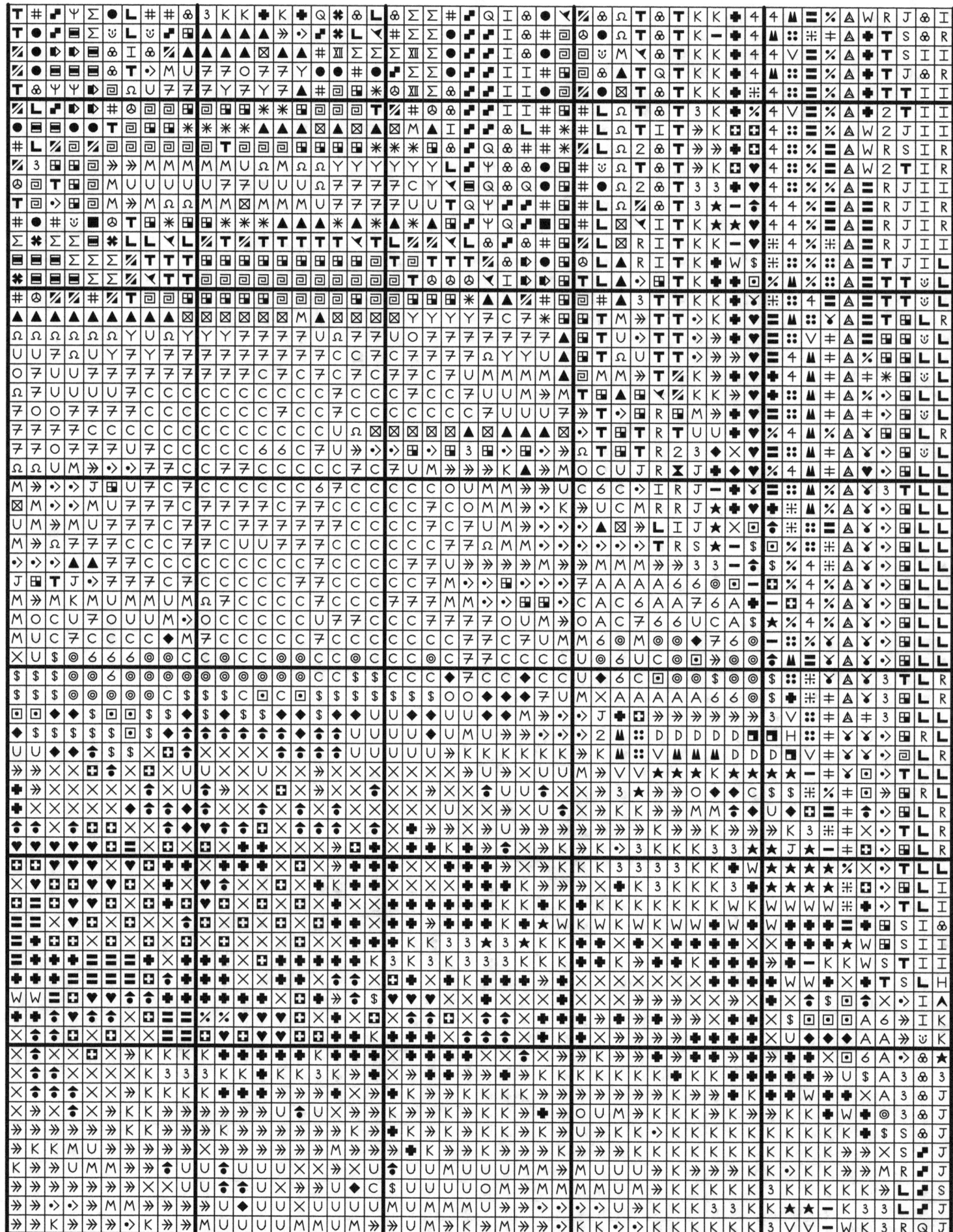

Street in Venice - Regular Print

Position D:4

Position A:5

Street in Venice - Regular Print

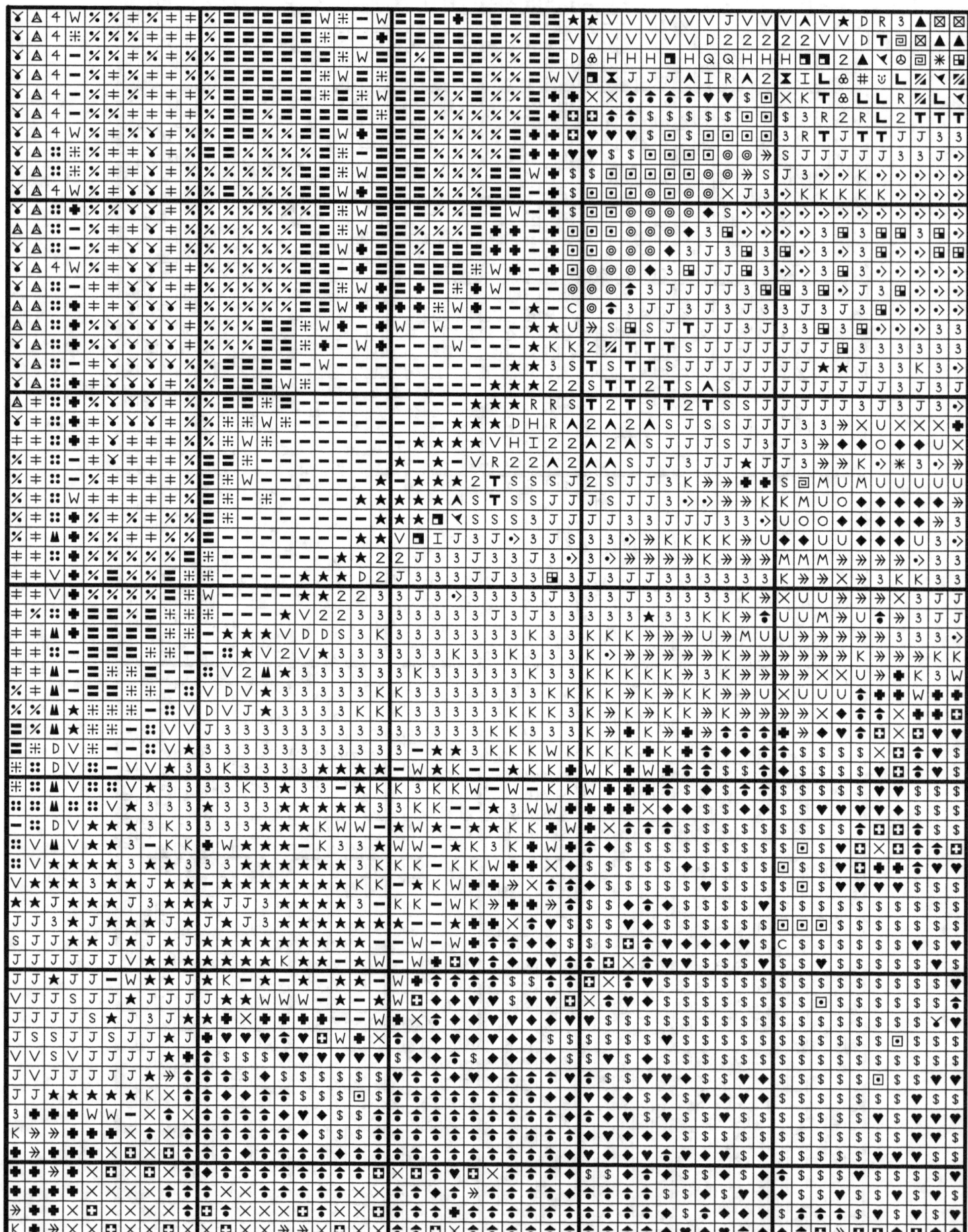

Position B:5　　　　　　　　　　　　　　　　　　　　　　　　　　　　　　　Street in Venice - Regular Print

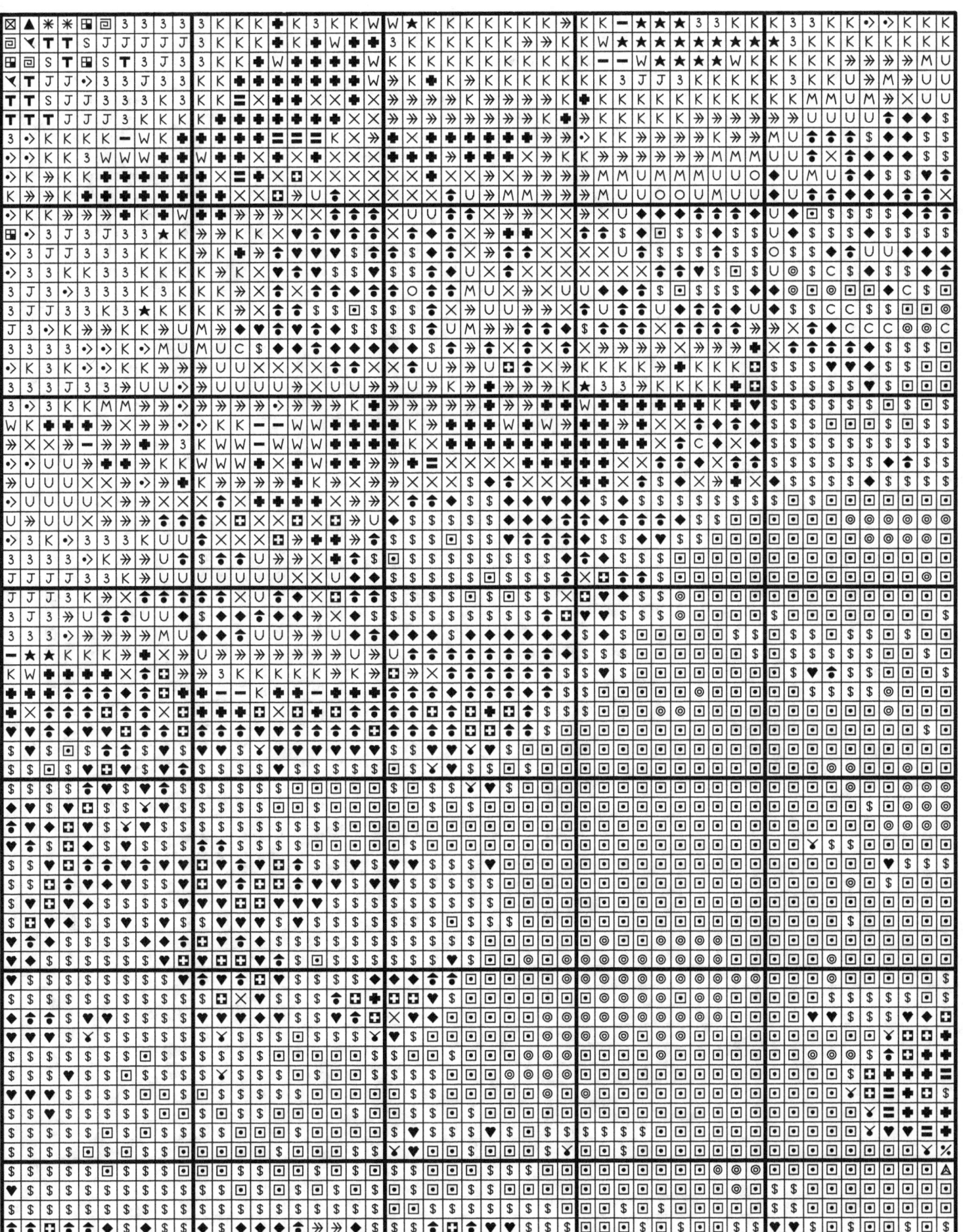

Position C:5 — Street in Venice - Regular Print

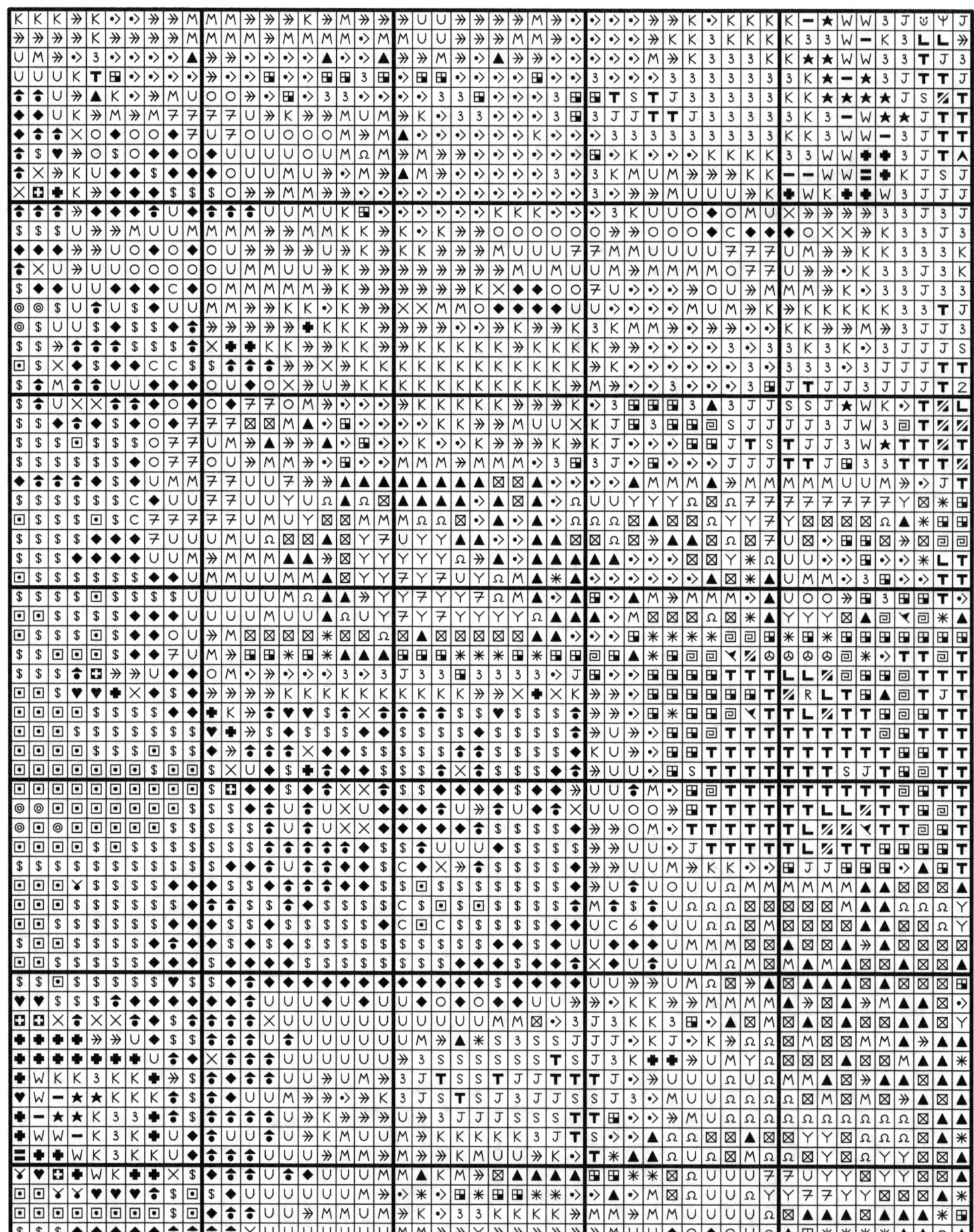

Position D:5 — Street in Venice - Regular Print

Large Print Chart

Street in Venice - Large Print

Overview

Fabric: Aida White

Stitch Count: 71/100mm or 18.0/inch

Chart Size: 189 x 324 Stitches

Finished Size: 267 x 457 mm or 10.5 x 18.0 inch

Fabric Size: 417 x 607 mm or 16.4 x 23.9 inch

Stitch Style: Cross stitch - 2 strands

Below is a plan showing how the chart pages fit together. The page number is shown at the top left of each chart page.

A:1	B:1	C:1	D:1	E:1
A:2	B:2	C:2	D:2	E:2
A:3	B:3	C:3	D:3	E:3
A:4	B:4	C:4	D:4	E:4
A:5	B:5	C:5	D:5	E:5
A:6	B:6	C:6	D:6	E:6
A:7	B:7	C:7	D:7	E:7

Position A:1 — Street in Venice - Large Print

Position B:1 — Street in Venice - Large Print

Position C:1 — Street in Venice - Large Print

Position D:1 — Street in Venice - Large Print

Position A:2 — Street in Venice - Large Print

Position B:2 — Street in Venice - Large Print

Position C:2 — Street in Venice - Large Print

Position D:2 — Street in Venice - Large Print

Position E:2 — Street in Venice - Large Print

Position A:3 — Street in Venice - Large Print

Position B:3 — Street in Venice - Large Print

Position C:3 — Street in Venice - Large Print

42

Position D:3 — Street in Venice - Large Print

Position E:3 — Street in Venice - Large Print

Position A:4 — Street in Venice - Large Print

Position B:4 — Street in Venice - Large Print

Position C:4 — Street in Venice - Large Print

Position D:4 — Street in Venice - Large Print

Position E:4 — Street in Venice - Large Print

Position A:5 — Street in Venice - Large Print

Position B:5 — Street in Venice - Large Print

Position C:5 — Street in Venice - Large Print

Position D:5 — Street in Venice - Large Print

Position E:5 — Street in Venice - Large Print

Position A:6 — Street in Venice - Large Print

Street in Venice - Large Print — Position B:6

Position C:6 — Street in Venice - Large Print

Position E:6 — Street in Venice - Large Print

Position A:7

Street in Venice - Large Print

Position B:7 — Street in Venice - Large Print

Position C:7 — Street in Venice - Large Print

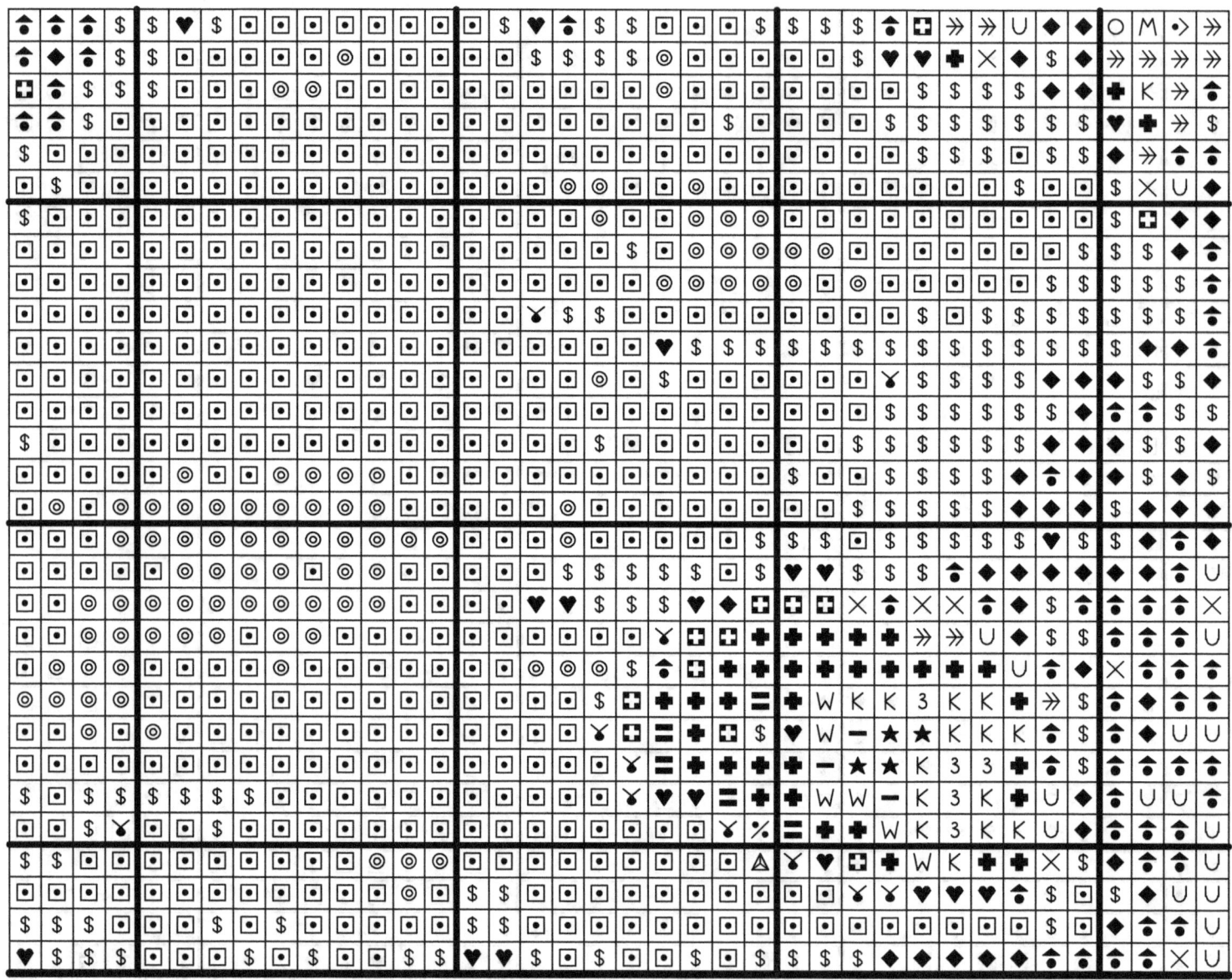

Position D:7 Street in Venice - Large Print

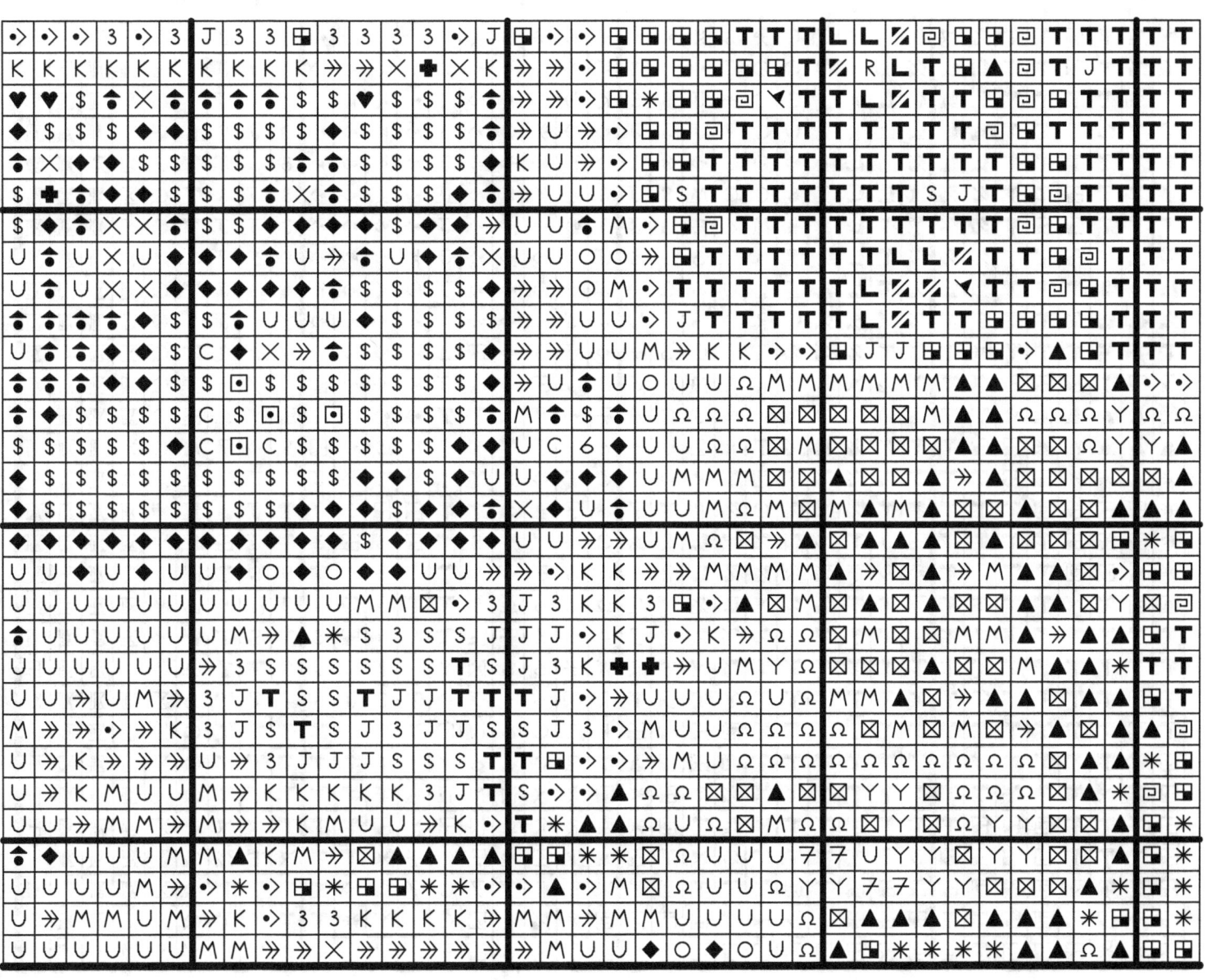

63

Position E:7 — Street in Venice - Large Print

Notes

www.ingramcontent.com/pod-product-compliance
Lightning Source LLC
Chambersburg PA
CBHW080526220526
45465CB00006B/2614